HOW TO SUCCEED IN TECH SUPPORT

A GUIDE TO THRIVING IN IT SUPPORT

NOE TOVAR-MBA

PUBLISHED BY
NOE TOVAR 2023
AMAZON

SCAN FOR AUTHOR PAGE TO ACCESS
OTHER BOOKS BY THIS AUTHOR

For more information, and other titles by this author please scan QR code on previous page.

ISBN: 9798861143967

Imprint: Independently published

Dedication

This book is dedicated to my family, whose unwavering support has been the bedrock of my journey, and to my friends, who have been both critics and confidants, thank you for being the pillars that held me up when the words threatened to crumble.

To the late nights and early mornings, to the moments of inspiration and the struggles of doubt, this dedication is a testament to the rollercoaster of emotions that accompanies the creation of every written word.

May this book serve as a token of gratitude to all those who have touched my life and inspired me to put my thoughts and experience to paper to share what I know and what stirs my curiosity. Your influence is woven into the very fabric of these pages, and I hope that the research, experience and personal thoughts within resonate with the same warmth and wonder that your presence has brought to my world.

With heartfelt appreciation,

With admiration and gratitude,

Noe Tovar-MBA

Table of Contents

WRITER'S NOTE

Writing "How to Succeed in Tech Support" has been a labor of love, born out of my passion for the world of technology and the countless experiences and lessons I've gathered throughout my career. While it seems like only yesterday I was standing in line overnight waiting to be one of the first to purchase windows 95. Allot has changed and it never stops changing.

In these pages, I've endeavored to distill the essence of what it takes to thrive in the dynamic field of tech support. I've drawn from personal experiences, insights shared by experts, and the ever-evolving landscape of the tech industry itself.

My hope is that this book serves as a valuable resource for both aspiring tech support professionals and those already immersed in this rewarding field. Whether you're just starting your journey or seeking to enhance your existing skills, the principles and strategies within these chapters can empower you to succeed.

Tech support is more than just solving technical issues; it's about building trust, fostering innovation, and making a positive impact on the lives of individuals and organizations. It's a field that continuously challenges and rewards those who are willing to embrace change, nurture their curiosity, and commit to lifelong learning.

As you embark on your own tech support odyssey, remember that the journey is uniquely yours. Your experiences, your challenges, and your triumphs will shape the professional you become. Embrace each opportunity to learn and grow, and know that the possibilities in tech support are as boundless as your determination and creativity.

I encourage you to approach this book with an open heart and an eager mind. Explore its pages, absorb its insights, and apply its wisdom to your own tech support journey. Whether you find inspiration in the words of experts or guidance in practical tips for success, my sincere wish is that this book empowers you to excel in the world of tech support.

Thank you for joining me on this literary adventure, and I wish you every success and fulfillment in your tech support endeavors.

Kind regards,

Noe Tovar-MBA

HOW TO SUCCEED IN TECH SUPPORT:

A GUIDE TO THRIVING IN IT SUPPORT

CHAPTER 1:
INTRODUCTION TO TECH SUPPORT

In the fast-paced, ever-evolving world of technology, the role of a tech support specialist is both indispensable and challenging. From troubleshooting hardware and software issues to helping users navigate complex systems, tech support professionals are the unsung heroes of the digital age. In this chapter, we'll delve into the fundamentals of tech support, its importance in today's society, and the fascinating journey that lies ahead for those aspiring to succeed in this field.

Understanding the Role of a
Tech Support Specialist

Tech support specialists, often referred to as IT support technicians or helpdesk agents, play a vital role in assisting individuals and organizations with their technology-related problems. Their responsibilities encompass a wide range of tasks, including:

- Problem Solving: The heart of tech support lies in identifying and resolving technical issues. Whether it's a malfunctioning printer, a software glitch, or a network outage, tech support specialists are the go-to experts for finding solutions.

- Customer Interaction: Effective communication is key in tech support. Specialists must listen attentively to users' concerns, ask probing questions, and provide clear instructions to help users navigate their tech challenges.

- Remote Support: With the advent of remote work and digital transformation, tech support often extends beyond physical office locations.

Specialists frequently provide assistance through remote desktop tools, phone calls, or chat interfaces.

- Documentation: Maintaining detailed records of issues, resolutions, and customer interactions is essential for tracking trends and improving service quality over time.

- Continuous Learning: In the world of technology, change is constant. Tech support professionals must stay updated with the latest hardware, software, and security trends to effectively address new challenges.

The Importance of Tech Support in the Digital Age

In an era where technology is intertwined with nearly every aspect of our lives, the importance of tech support cannot be overstated. Consider the following scenarios:

- Business Continuity: Organizations rely on technology to operate efficiently. Downtime due to technical issues can lead to significant financial losses. Tech support ensures that businesses can maintain their operations smoothly.

- User Productivity: Individual users, whether at home or in the office, depend on technology to perform their daily tasks. When technical problems arise, they can disrupt productivity and cause frustration.

- Cybersecurity: With the growing threat of cyberattacks, tech support plays a critical role in identifying and mitigating security risks. Specialists help protect sensitive data and prevent data breaches.

- Innovation: Tech support isn't just about fixing what's broken; it's also about enabling innovation. By assisting users in adopting new technologies and software, tech support fuels progress.

The Evolution of Tech Support

Tech support has come a long way since its inception. In the early days of computing, it often involved simple tasks like replacing hardware components or reinstalling software. However, as technology has advanced, so too has the complexity of tech support.

Today, tech support encompasses a broad spectrum of services, from troubleshooting common issues to handling intricate cloud infrastructure problems. The emergence of remote support tools, artificial intelligence, and automation has transformed the way support is delivered.

As we progress through this book, you'll discover the essential skills, tools, and strategies that will empower you to excel in the dynamic and rewarding field of tech support. Whether you're just starting your tech support journey or seeking to enhance your existing skills, this guide will provide you with the knowledge and insights needed to succeed in this ever-evolving industry. So, let's embark on this journey together and uncover the secrets to becoming a tech support superstar.

Key Topics for IT Support Engineers

 **Operating Systems**

Learning about Windows and Linux basics for troubleshooting.

 Networking Fundamentals

Understanding IP addresses, DNS. DHCP. and ol concept of subnetting.

 **Hardware Support**

Knowing deskto; and laptop components like printers and peripherals,

 **Software Support**

Assisting with Microsoft Office, web browsers and emall clients.

 Active Directory

Managing user accounts. permissions, and group policies.

 **Basic Cyber secururity**

Practicing safe behavior, phishing awareness, and endpoint protection.

 System Backup & Imaging

Understand tools and techniques for system, recovery.

Soft Skills

CHAPTER 2:
ESSENTIAL SKILLS FOR TECH SUPPORT

Tech support is more than just knowing how to fix technical issues; it's about possessing a unique set of skills that enable you to excel in this dynamic field. In this chapter, we will explore the core skills that every successful tech support specialist should cultivate. Whether you are just starting your career or looking to enhance your existing abilities, understanding and honing these skills will be crucial to your success.

1. Technical Proficiency

At the heart of tech support is a deep understanding of technology. This includes:

- Operating Systems: Proficiency in popular operating systems such as Windows, macOS, and Linux.

- Hardware Knowledge: Familiarity with computer components, peripherals, and networking hardware.

- Software Expertise: A broad understanding of software applications, from office suites to specialized software relevant to your field.

- Troubleshooting Skills: The ability to diagnose and resolve a wide range of technical issues efficiently.

- Scripting and Coding: Basic knowledge of scripting languages (e.g., PowerShell, Python) can be a valuable asset for automating repetitive tasks.

2. Problem-Solving Skills

Tech support is essentially about solving puzzles. Your problem-solving skills should encompass:

- Critical Thinking: The capacity to analyze complex problems, break them down into manageable components, and develop effective solutions.

- Logical Reasoning: The ability to follow logical steps and methodologies to identify the root cause of an issue.

- Creativity: Sometimes, unconventional solutions are required. Being creative in your approach can lead to innovative problem-solving.

3. Communication Skills

Effective communication is fundamental in tech support, as you'll often interact with individuals who may not share your technical knowledge. Key communication skills include:

- Active Listening: Paying full attention to the user's problem, asking clarifying questions, and showing empathy.

- Clear and Concise Communication: Explaining technical concepts and solutions in plain language, avoiding jargon.

- Written Communication: Craft well-structured and detailed documentation for troubleshooting steps, FAQs, and knowledge base articles.

4. Patience and Empathy

Tech support can be frustrating for both you and the users you assist. Patience and empathy are vital for maintaining a positive customer experience. Recognizing the user's frustration and providing empathetic support can go a long way in resolving issues efficiently.

5. Time Management

In tech support, time is often of the essence. Balancing multiple requests and prioritizing tasks is crucial. Effective time management ensures that you can respond to urgent issues promptly without neglecting long-term projects or proactive support.

6. Adaptability

The tech landscape is ever-changing. New technologies, software updates, and security threats continually emerge. Adaptability allows you to stay current and agile in addressing new challenges and learning new skills.

These skills are the foundation of your success in tech support. As you progress in your career, you'll continue to refine and expand upon these abilities. The next chapters of this book will delve deeper into each of these skills, providing practical advice and real-world examples to help you become a tech support specialist who not only solves technical problems but also exceeds customer expectations and contributes to the success of your organization.

Key Skills for IT Support Technicians

CHAPTER 3:
BUILDING A STRONG FOUNDATION

When I embarked on my journey in tech support, I quickly realized that a strong foundation was the key to success in this dynamic and ever-evolving field. In this chapter, I'll share my experiences and insights on how to build that essential foundation, from education and certifications to practical hands-on learning.

Educational Background and Certifications

My journey into tech support began with a passion for technology and problem-solving. While a formal education is not always a prerequisite for entering this field, it can certainly provide a solid foundation. Here are some steps I took and lessons I learned:

- Choose Your Path: Decide on your area of interest within tech support. It could be general IT support, network support, security, or specialized support for specific software or hardware.

- Pursue Relevant Education: Consider enrolling in courses or pursuing a degree in computer science, information technology, or a related field. These programs provide a structured curriculum and foundational knowledge.

- Certifications Matter: Certifications are your ticket to proving your expertise. Certifications from CompTIA (e.g., A+, Network+, Security+), Microsoft (e.g., MCSA, MCSE), Cisco (e.g., CCNA, CCNP), and other industry-recognized organizations can open doors and demonstrate your commitment to the profession.

- Hands-On Experience: While education and certifications provide a strong base, nothing beats hands-on experience. Set up a home lab environment where you can experiment, break things, and learn from your mistakes without the pressure of real-world consequences.

Building a Personal Lab

Creating a personal lab was one of the best decisions I made early in my tech support journey. It allowed me to explore various technologies, simulate real-world scenarios, and gain practical experience. Here's how you can set up your own lab:

- Select the Hardware: You don't need expensive equipment. Start with a decent computer, a router, and virtualization software like VMware Workstation or VirtualBox.

- Install Virtual Machines (VMs): Create VMs to mimic different operating systems and network configurations. This will enable you to practice troubleshooting and testing without affecting your primary system.

- Experiment and Learn: Use your lab to experiment with different setups, software installations, and configurations. Try breaking things and then fixing them.

- Documentation: Keep detailed notes of your lab setups, configurations, and troubleshooting steps. This will become a valuable resource as you encounter similar issues in the real world.

Staying Current with Technology Trends

The tech world never stands still, and neither should you. Staying current with technology trends is crucial for success in tech support. Here's how I managed to stay up-to-date:

- Continuous Learning: Make learning a lifelong habit. Read tech blogs, follow industry news, and engage in online forums and communities.

- Professional Development: Attend workshops, webinars, and conferences to gain insights into emerging technologies and best practices.

- Networking: Build a network of peers and mentors in the industry. Sharing experiences and knowledge with others can be invaluable.

- Certification Renewal: Most certifications require regular renewal, which often involves continuing education. Embrace this as an opportunity to deepen your skills.

- Hands-On Practice: Whenever possible, implement new technologies or software in your lab environment. Practical experience reinforces your understanding.

Building a strong foundation in tech support is not a one-time effort but a continuous journey. Whether you're starting from scratch or looking to enhance your existing skills, remember that the knowledge and experience you gain will not only boost your confidence but also set you on a path to becoming a respected and sought-after tech support specialist. The adventure has just begun, and the next chapters will delve deeper into the practical aspects of excelling in this field.

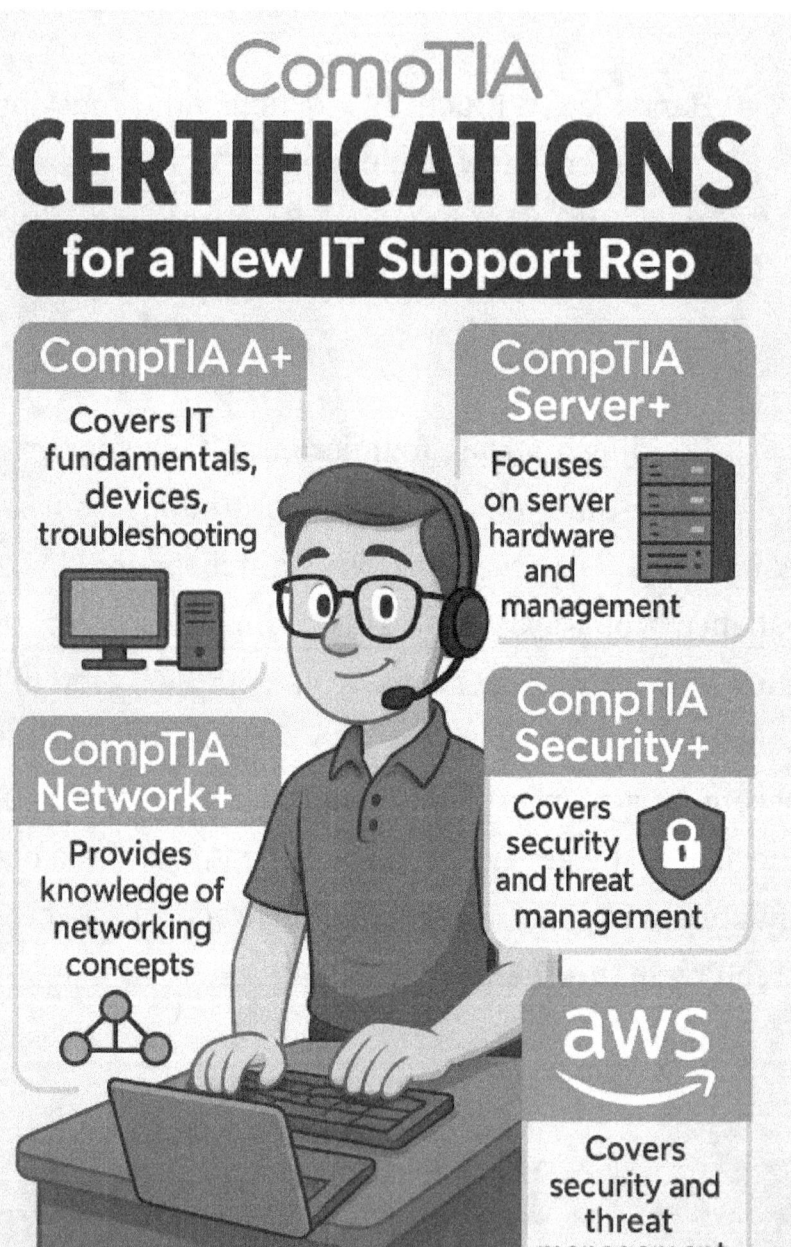

CHAPTER 4:
THE ART OF TROUBLESHOOTING

As I progressed in my tech support journey, I discovered that troubleshooting is at the heart of what we do. It's the process of identifying, diagnosing, and ultimately resolving technical issues—a puzzle that requires patience, critical thinking, and creativity. In this chapter, I'll share my experiences and insights into the art of troubleshooting, a skill every tech support specialist must master.

The Problem-Solving Process

Successful troubleshooting follows a structured problem-solving process. Here's a breakdown of the steps I've found to be effective:

- Identifying and Defining the Problem:

- *Start by listening carefully to the user's description of the issue.*

- *Ask questions to gather more information and clarify the problem's symptoms.*

- *Create a clear and concise problem statement.*

- Research and Documentation:

- *Consult documentation, manuals, and knowledge bases to see if there are known solutions.*

- *Document your findings and the steps you've taken so far.*

- Analyzing Possible Solutions:

- *Brainstorm potential solutions based on your understanding of the problem.*

- *Prioritize solutions by considering their feasibility and potential impact.*

- Testing and Implementing Solutions:

- *Begin with the simplest and least disruptive solutions.*

- *Test each solution methodically, documenting the outcomes.*

- *If a solution works, great! If not, revert the changes and try the next solution.*

- Follow-Up and Continuous Improvement:

- *Check back with the user to ensure the issue is resolved and get their feedback.*

- *Review the troubleshooting process and consider what could have been done differently or more efficiently for future reference.*

Real-World Troubleshooting Scenarios

Throughout my tech support career, I've encountered a wide range of troubleshooting scenarios. Here are a few examples that highlight the diverse challenges you might face:

- Software Crashes: A user's application crashes without warning. You must determine if it's a software conflict, a corrupt installation, or something else entirely.

- Network Connectivity Issues: Users report intermittent internet connectivity problems. Troubleshooting may involve diagnosing hardware, configuring routers, or identifying interference sources.

- Data Loss: A user accidentally deletes critical files. Here, the challenge is data recovery, whether from backups or using specialized tools.

- Blue Screen of Death (BSOD): An infamous Windows error that can have numerous causes, from hardware issues to faulty drivers. Identifying the root cause requires careful examination.

- Email Delivery Problems: Emails aren't reaching their intended recipients. You might need to investigate email server configurations, DNS records, or spam filters.

Each of these scenarios requires a unique approach, but the problem-solving process remains the same. You'll need to adapt your troubleshooting skills to the specific situation, utilizing your technical knowledge, research abilities, and communication skills effectively.

Documentation: Your Troubleshooting Companion

One of the most valuable tools in troubleshooting is documentation. Whenever you encounter an issue and work towards a resolution, it's crucial to document your steps, findings, and the final solution. This documentation serves several purposes:

- *Reference for Future Issues: Similar issues may arise in the future, and your documentation can serve as a reference to expedite resolutions.*

- *Knowledge Sharing: If you work in a team, well-documented troubleshooting processes can be shared with colleagues, ensuring consistent support.*

- *Self-Improvement: Reviewing your documentation allows you to learn from past experiences and refine your troubleshooting techniques.*

The art of troubleshooting is a skill that develops over time. With each issue you encounter and solve, you gain valuable experience and confidence. Remember that, as a tech support specialist, you are not expected to have all the answers instantly, but you are expected to be resourceful, patient, and persistent in your pursuit of solutions.

In the next chapters, we'll explore more specific aspects of tech support, from effective communication with users to the tools and technologies that can make your troubleshooting efforts even more efficient.

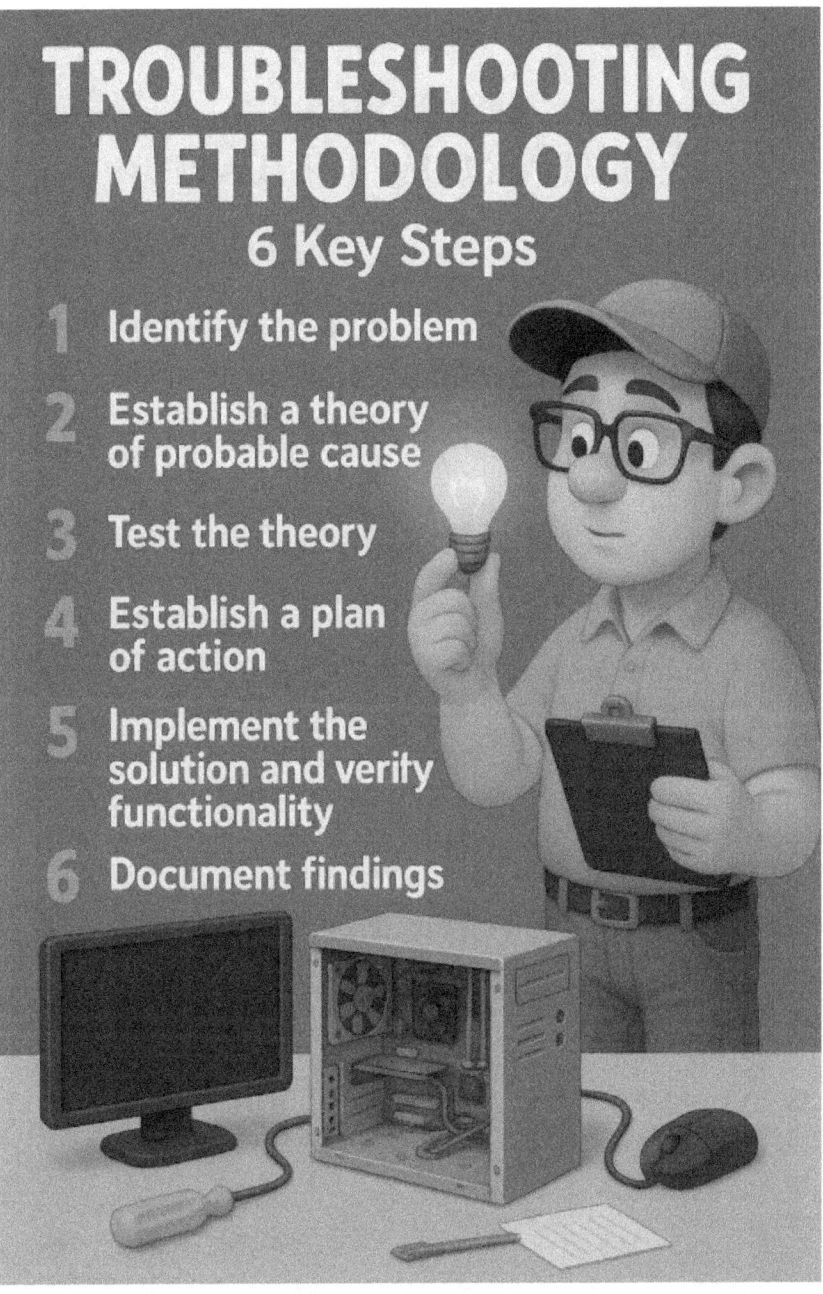

CHAPTER 5:
EFFECTIVE COMMUNICATION

"Your ability to communicate is an important tool in your pursuit of your goals, whether it is with your family, your co-workers, or your clients and customers."

— Les Brown

Les Brown's words resonate deeply with me as I reflect on my journey in tech support. Effective communication isn't just a skill; it's a superpower that can make or break your success in this field. In this chapter, I want to share my personal insights, infused with my unique personality, on the vital role communication plays in tech support.

The Expert's Wisdom

Before we dive into my experiences, let's draw inspiration from an expert in the field of communication: Les Brown. His expertise in motivational speaking and communication is a goldmine of wisdom. One of his key teachings is the power of belief in oneself and the ability to convey that belief to others. In tech support, this translates into the confidence you project when addressing users' issues.

Here are a few takeaways from Les Brown's teachings, adapted to the world of tech support:

- *Believe in Your Expertise: Have confidence in your skills and knowledge. Users are more likely to trust and follow your guidance when they sense your expertise.*

- *Positive Attitude: Maintain a positive and enthusiastic attitude, even when dealing with challenging issues. Your optimism can be contagious and reassuring to users.*

- *Authenticity: Be your authentic self. Authenticity fosters trust and genuine connections with users.*

Now, let's explore how to apply these principles and my own experiences in effective tech support communication:

Active Listening: The Bedrock of Effective Communication

Imagine this: A user contacts you with a frustrating technical issue. They're upset, and their frustration is palpable. In this scenario, active listening is your secret weapon.

When I'm faced with a distressed user, I take a deep breath and remind myself to practice active listening:

- *Give Your Full Attention: I clear my mind of distractions and focus solely on the user's words. This makes them feel heard and valued.*

- *Empathize and Validate: I acknowledge their frustration and express empathy. Simple phrases like "I understand how frustrating this must be" can go a long way.*

- *Ask Clarifying Questions: I ask open-ended questions to gather more information and ensure I fully grasp the issue. This not only helps in troubleshooting but also reassures the user that I care about resolving their problem.*

Clear and Concise Communication: Break It Down

Tech jargon can be a daunting barrier for users. That's where clear and concise communication comes into play:

- *Plain Language: I avoid using technical jargon whenever possible. Instead, I explain concepts and solutions in everyday language.*

- *Step-by-Step Guidance: When providing instructions, I break them down into simple, sequential steps. I often ask users to follow along as I guide them through the process.*

- *Visual Aids: A picture is worth a thousand words. I use screenshots, diagrams, and screen sharing to visually illustrate solutions when necessary.*

Handling Difficult Customers: Keep Your Cool

Dealing with irate or frustrated customers is par for the course in tech support. Here's how I handle such situations while staying true to my personality:

- *Maintain a Calm Demeanor: I keep my cool, reminding myself not to take their frustration personally.*

- *Empathize Sincerely: I genuinely empathize with their situation and express understanding of their emotions.*

- *Offer Solutions, Not Excuses: I focus on finding solutions rather than dwelling on who or what caused the problem. I believe in fixing it first and discussing the cause later.*

- *Use Humor Wisely: Injecting a touch of humor can sometimes lighten the mood, but it's crucial to use it judiciously and with sensitivity.*

Effective communication isn't just about conveying technical information; it's about building trust and rapport with users. When users feel understood and valued, their tech support experience becomes not just a problem-solving session but a positive interaction.

In the next chapter, we'll explore the tools and technologies that can amplify your communication and support capabilities, all while staying true to your unique personality and style.

CHAPTER 6:
TOOLS OF THE TRADE

As I progressed in my tech support journey, I quickly learned that having the right tools at my disposal was essential for success in this field. In this chapter, I'll share my personal experiences with the tools and software that have become indispensable in my tech support arsenal.

Common Tech Support Software

In the fast-paced world of tech support, having the right software can make all the difference. Here are some of the common software tools that have proven invaluable:

- *Remote Desktop Tools: When providing remote support, tools like TeamViewer, AnyDesk, or*

Remote Desktop Protocol (RDP) enable you to access and troubleshoot users' systems from a distance.

- *Troubleshooting Utilities: Software like PuTTY (for SSH and Telnet), Wireshark (for network analysis), and Process Explorer (for in-depth process management) can help you diagnose and resolve technical issues efficiently.*

- *Help Desk Software: Tools like Zendesk, Freshdesk, or ServiceNow are essential for managing and tracking support tickets, ensuring nothing falls through the cracks.*

- *Screen Recording and Capture: Snagit or OBS Studio can be used to record video tutorials or capture screenshots, which are valuable for documenting solutions or creating knowledge base articles.*

- *Remote Monitoring and Management (RMM) Software: If you're in a managed IT services role,*

RMM platforms like ConnectWise Automate or SolarWinds RMM can help you proactively manage and monitor client systems.

Remote Desktop Tools: Bridging the Distance

One of the most transformative tools I've used in tech support is remote desktop software. It allows you to virtually step into a user's environment, see the issue firsthand, and troubleshoot as if you were physically present. Here's how it has enhanced my support capabilities:

- *Efficiency: Remote desktop tools significantly reduce resolution time by eliminating the need for users to describe issues verbally. I can see exactly what's happening on their screen.*

- Training and Guidance: These tools are invaluable for providing step-by-step guidance.

I can demonstrate solutions in real time, enhancing user understanding.

- Minimizing Disruption: Users can continue working while I troubleshoot in the background, reducing downtime and disruption to their tasks.

Troubleshooting Hardware: The Physical Side of Support

Hardware issues are a common part of tech support, and having the right tools for diagnosing and fixing hardware problems is crucial. Here are some hardware troubleshooting tools I've relied on:

- *Multi-meter: A versatile tool for testing electrical currents, voltages, and resistances, making it essential for diagnosing hardware failures.*

- *Screwdriver Set: A good set of precision screwdrivers is a must for opening up computers and other hardware devices for repair or maintenance.*

- *Cable Testers: These are used to check the integrity of network and data cables, identifying faults or connectivity issues.*

- *USB Drive with Portable Diagnostic Tools: I keep a bootable USB drive with diagnostic software like MemTest86, SpinRite, and Hiren's BootCD for diagnosing and repairing hardware problems.*

Creating and Managing Knowledge Bases

Knowledge is power, and in tech support, knowledge bases are your repository of power. I've found that maintaining a well-organized knowledge base is essential for efficient support. Here's how it has helped me:

- *Quick Reference: A well-structured knowledge base provides quick access to common issues and solutions, reducing research time.*

- *Consistency: It ensures that support staff provide consistent and accurate information to users.*

- *Training and Onboarding: New support team members can quickly get up to speed by referencing the knowledge base.*

- *Self-Help for Users: A well-maintained knowledge base can also empower users to resolve common issues independently.*

Ticketing Systems: Keeping Things Organized

When dealing with a high volume of support requests, ticketing systems are a lifesaver. They help in tracking, prioritizing, and managing support requests efficiently. The ability to assign tickets, set due dates, and provide status updates ensures nothing falls through the cracks.

In my tech support journey, I've discovered that the right tools not only improve efficiency but also enhance the quality of support provided. Whether it's remote desktop software, hardware diagnostics, knowledge base systems, or ticketing platforms, these tools are the backbone of a successful tech support operation.

In the next chapter, we'll explore the importance of time management and prioritization in tech support, and how these skills can further enhance your support capabilities.

RECOMMENDED TOOLS FOR TECH SUPPORT

Headset
for communication

Laptop
for remote access

Webcam
for video calls

CHAPTER 7:
TIME MANAGEMENT AND PRIORITIZATION

Throughout my career in tech support, I've come to understand that time is one of our most valuable resources. How we manage it can significantly impact our effectiveness and the level of support we provide. In this chapter, I'll share my experiences and the wisdom of an expert in the field, Brian Tracy, on the importance of time management and prioritization.

The Expert's Lesson: Brian Tracy on Time Management

Brian Tracy, a renowned author and motivational speaker, once said, "Every minute you spend in planning saves 10 minutes in execution." His words emphasize the profound impact of effective time management on productivity and success. This lesson has resonated with me throughout my tech support journey.

Here are some key takeaways from Brian Tracy's teachings on time management, adapted to the world of tech support:

- *Set Clear Goals: Begin with a clear understanding of your goals for the day or week. What support tasks need your attention, and what outcomes do you aim to achieve?*

- *Prioritize Ruthlessly: Not all support requests are created equal. Identify high-priority tasks and focus on them first. Often, resolving one critical issue can alleviate multiple smaller ones.*

- *Plan and Schedule: Create a structured schedule that allocates time for different types of support tasks, including reactive support (responding to user requests) and proactive support (maintenance, updates, and knowledge base improvement).*

- *Avoid Multitasking: Contrary to popular belief, multitasking can decrease efficiency. It's often more productive to concentrate on one task at a time.*

Now, let's explore how these principles and my own experiences have shaped my approach to time management and prioritization in tech support:

Managing Workload: The Art of Balancing Act

Tech support often involves juggling multiple tasks, from addressing user inquiries and troubleshooting issues to performing system updates and maintaining documentation. Here's what I've learned about managing workload effectively:

- *Prioritization: Start your day by identifying and prioritizing tasks. Tackle high-priority items first to ensure critical issues are addressed promptly.*

- *Setting Realistic Expectations: Communicate realistic timelines to users. Under-promise and over-deliver, rather than making lofty commitments that may not be achievable.*

- *Time Blocking: Allocate specific blocks of time for different types of tasks. For instance, set aside uninterrupted time for proactive work and reserve another block for addressing reactive support requests.*

Balancing Reactive and Proactive Support

Reactive support, such as responding to user inquiries and resolving urgent issues, often takes center stage in tech support. However, proactive support is equally vital. It involves activities like system maintenance, updates, and knowledge base enhancement. Here's how I've struck a balance:

- *Time Allocation: Dedicate a portion of your schedule to proactive tasks. Neglecting them can lead to technical debt and more reactive support in the long run.*

- *Automation: Identify repetitive tasks that can be automated. Automation tools can save you considerable time and effort, allowing you to focus on more complex support issues.*

Handling Multiple Tasks and Requests

The tech support queue can become overwhelming at times. Here's how I've managed to handle multiple tasks and requests effectively:

Ticket Management: Ticketing systems are your allies in managing and prioritizing requests. Use them to categorize, assign, and track support tickets.

Effective Communication: If you're working on multiple issues simultaneously, communicate clearly with users about your progress and expected resolution times.

- Delegation: In larger support teams, delegation becomes crucial. Delegate tasks based on team members' expertise to ensure efficient handling of requests.

- *Tech support is a dynamic field that requires adaptability and effective time management. By applying the principles of goal setting, prioritization, planning, and focus, I've learned to optimize my productivity and provide quality support to users.*

- *In the next chapter, we'll explore the human element in tech support, including teamwork, collaboration, mentoring, and strategies for dealing with stress and burnout—crucial aspects of a fulfilling career in this field.*

CHAPTER 8:
THE HUMAN ELEMENT

As we journey through the world of tech support, we've explored various facets of this dynamic field, from technical proficiency and communication skills to time management and the human side of support. In this final chapter, I want to reflect on our journey together and explore the endless possibilities and opportunities that lie ahead in the world of tech support.

A Lesson from the Expert: Sheryl Sandberg on Resilience

Sheryl Sandberg, the Chief Operating Officer of Facebook and author of "Lean In," has shared invaluable insights on resilience. She has taught us that resilience is not about avoiding adversity but about navigating through it and emerging stronger on the other side. This lesson has resonated deeply with me in my tech support journey.

Here are some key takeaways from Sheryl Sandberg's teachings on resilience and how they apply to the future of tech support:

- *Face Challenges Head-On: Embrace challenges as opportunities for growth. In tech support, this means viewing complex technical issues as chances to expand your knowledge and problem-solving skills.*

- *Learn from Failure: Resilience involves learning from failures and setbacks. In tech support, not every problem can be solved instantly, but each encounter is a chance to refine your approach and knowledge.*

Now, let's delve into the future of tech support, equipped with the lessons we've learned on our journey:

The Evolving Landscape of Tech Support

The tech support landscape is continually evolving, driven by advancements in technology and changes in user expectations. Here are some key trends and developments that are shaping the future of tech support:

- *AI and Automation: Artificial intelligence (AI) and automation are becoming integral to tech support. Chatbots and virtual assistants can handle routine inquiries, freeing up human specialists to focus on more complex issues.*

- *Remote Support: Remote work is here to stay, and tech support has adapted accordingly. Remote support tools and practices have become essential for addressing user issues from afar.*

- *Data-Driven Support: Analyzing support data can provide insights into common issues and areas for improvement. This data-driven approach allows organizations to proactively address recurring problems.*

- *Personalization: Users expect personalized support experiences. Tech support is increasingly tailored to individual needs, with context-aware solutions and recommendations.*

- *Self-Service Options: Knowledge bases, FAQs, and user forums empower users to find solutions independently. Tech support specialists are now often tasked with creating and maintaining these resources.*

The Role of the Tech Support Specialist

As tech support continues to evolve, the role of the tech support specialist will also change. Here are some skills and qualities that will be increasingly valuable:

- *Adaptability: Tech support specialists must stay current with ever-changing technology trends and be flexible in adapting to new tools and methodologies.*

- *Data Literacy: Understanding and analyzing support data will be essential for identifying trends and improving the support process.*

- *Empathy and Soft Skills: As automation takes over routine tasks, the human touch becomes even more critical. Empathy and effective communication will remain invaluable.*

- *Continuous Learning: The learning journey doesn't end in tech support. Specialists must remain committed to ongoing education and skill development.*

Endless Opportunities

The world of tech support is full of endless opportunities for those who are willing to embrace change and continue learning. Whether you aspire to become a technical expert in a specific field, explore leadership roles, or dive into the exciting realms of AI-driven support, the future is bright.

But remember, resilience, as Sheryl Sandberg teaches us, is key. Challenges will arise, and you may face setbacks, but each experience will only make you stronger and more capable.

As we conclude our journey through the world of tech support, I encourage you to keep learning, adapting, and embracing the future with an open mind and a willingness to grow. The world of tech support is yours to shape, and I have no doubt that you will leave your mark on this ever-evolving field. Thank you for joining me on this adventure, and I wish you a fulfilling and successful career in tech support.

CompTIA
RECOMMENDED SOFT SKILLS

Communication

Calm an irate customer
by listening and asking qus

Professionalism

Maintain positive attitude
and show respect

Problem Solving

Ask questions and
troubleshoot to resolve issues

Adaptability

Be willing to learn new
technologies and procedures

CHAPTER 9:
A JOURNEY OF ENDLESS POSSIBILITIES

In the previous chapter, we explored the ever-evolving landscape of tech support and the vital role of resilience in navigating through challenges. As we conclude our journey together, I want to share some final thoughts on the limitless possibilities that await those who embark on a career in tech support. And to guide us, let's draw inspiration from an expert, Steve Jobs, who left an indelible mark on the tech industry.

A Lesson from the Expert: Steve Jobs on Innovation

Steve Jobs, the co-founder of Apple Inc. and a pioneer in the tech world, once said, "Innovation distinguishes between a leader and a follower." His relentless pursuit of innovation transformed the way we interact with technology. From him, we learn that innovation is not just about creating new products but also about constantly improving processes and approaches. This lesson has profound relevance in the tech support domain.

Here are some key takeaways from Steve Jobs' teachings on innovation and how they apply to tech support:

- *Challenge the Status Quo: Don't settle for "this is how we've always done it." Question assumptions and seek better ways to provide support.*

- *User-Centric Approach: Innovation in tech support means putting the user's needs and experience at the forefront. How can we make the support journey smoother, faster, and more satisfying?*

Now, let's explore the endless possibilities in tech support:

The Ongoing Evolution of Tech Support

Tech support is a field that never stands still. It constantly adapts to new technologies, user behaviors, and expectations. Here are some areas where we can expect continued evolution:

- *Artificial Intelligence and Automation: AI-driven chatbots, virtual assistants, and automation will play a more prominent role in handling routine support tasks, allowing human specialists to focus on complex issues.*

- *Data-Driven Insights: The analysis of support data will become even more sophisticated, providing organizations with valuable insights for continuous improvement.*

- *Personalization: Support experiences will be increasingly tailored to individual users, delivering more relevant solutions.*

- *Remote Support: As remote work becomes more prevalent, remote support tools and practices will continue to evolve.*

The Future Tech Support Specialist

As tech support evolves, so will the role of the tech support specialist. Here's how:

- *Adaptive Skills: Specialists will need to adapt to new tools, technologies, and methodologies continually.*

- *Strategic Thinking: Beyond solving immediate issues, tech support specialists will play a more strategic role in improving overall support processes and enhancing the user experience.*

- *Global Collaboration: With remote work, tech support teams may become more distributed, requiring effective collaboration across time zones and cultures.*

Unleash Your Innovative Spirit

As you embark on your tech support career or continue your journey in this field, remember that innovation is not limited to product development— it's a mindset and an approach. Embrace change, challenge the status quo, and always seek ways to improve.

Don't be afraid to propose innovative solutions, whether it's streamlining support processes, enhancing self-help resources, or creating new tools to empower users. Your innovative spirit can not only improve your effectiveness as a tech support specialist but also contribute to the broader advancement of the field.

Conclusion: Your Tech Support Odyssey

Our journey through the world of tech support has been an exploration of knowledge, skills, and experiences. From technical proficiency and communication to time management, empathy, and innovation, we've delved into the many facets of this dynamic field.

As you move forward, remember that tech support is not just a job; it's a continuous odyssey of learning and growth. Each interaction with a user, each technical challenge, and each new technological development is an opportunity to expand your expertise and make a meaningful impact.

So, set forth on your tech support odyssey with confidence, resilience, and an unwavering commitment to excellence. The possibilities are endless, and the journey is yours to shape. Thank you for joining me on this adventure, and I wish you a fulfilling and successful career in tech support, filled with innovation, compassion, and endless possibilities.

CHAPTER 10:
THE POWER OF LIFELONG LEARNING

As we wrap up our journey through the world of tech support, I can't help but reflect on the incredible insights and experiences we've shared. From technical expertise to communication skills, resilience, and the importance of embracing change and innovation, it's been a thrilling adventure.

Transition from the Previous Chapter

In the last chapter, we drew inspiration from Albert Einstein's wisdom on lifelong learning, emphasizing that intellectual growth should continue throughout our lives. Now, in this final chapter, I want to delve deeper into the profound significance of lifelong learning in the tech support field, where change is not just constant; it's the very essence of our work.

The Lifelong Learning Imperative

Tech support, as we've seen, is a dynamic field where evolution is the norm. New technologies emerge, user expectations shift, and novel challenges surface regularly. To not just survive but thrive in this ever-changing landscape, lifelong learning isn't merely a suggestion; it's an absolute necessity.

Let's explore why continuous learning is pivotal in tech support:

- *Staying Current: The tech industry evolves at a breathtaking pace. New software, hardware, and best practices appear almost daily. Keeping up with these changes is crucial to delivering top-notch support.*

- *Adaptation: As support processes and tools undergo metamorphosis, you must adapt to them. Learning to wield new support software or*

*understanding   emerging   technologies   is
essential.*

- *Problem-Solving Mastery: Each support request is a riddle, waiting for your expert touch. The more you learn and expand your knowledge base, the better equipped you are to decipher these puzzles effectively.*

Lifelong Learning in Practice

So, how can you incorporate lifelong learning into your tech support journey? Here are some practical approaches to keep the flame of curiosity burning:

- *Online Courses and Certifications: There's a vast array of online courses and certifications available in various tech-related fields. Consider pursuing these to deepen your knowledge.*

- *Professional Organizations: Joining tech support or IT-related professional organizations opens doors to resources, networking opportunities, and educational events.*

- *Blogs and Forums: Tech blogs, online forums, and industry news sources are treasure troves of information about the latest trends and developments.*

- *Mentorship: Seek out mentors within your organization or industry. Learning from experienced professionals can be an invaluable part of your journey.*

The Journey Continues

As we wrap up our exploration of tech support, I want to leave you with this thought: your journey in this field is far from over—it's just beginning. Tech support offers boundless opportunities for those who are willing to embrace lifelong learning, adapt to change, and keep their curiosity alive.

Whether you aspire to become a technical expert, a team leader, or a pioneer in AI-driven support, remember that your journey is unique, and the possibilities are limitless.

Thank you for joining me on this adventure through the world of tech support. As you continue to grow, learn, and make your mark in this dynamic field, remember that your journey of lifelong learning has the power to reshape the tech support landscape and drive innovation for years to come.

CompTIA
CERTIFICATIONS
FOR A NEW IT SUPPORT REP

CompTIA A+

Foundational IT skills

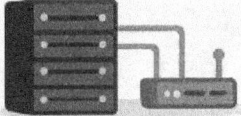

CompTIA Server+

Administering servers

CompTIA Network+

Configuring and managing networks

CompTIA Security+

Working with AWS cloud services

CHAPTER 11:
PRACTICAL TIPS FOR SUCCESS IN TECH SUPPORT

Throughout my journey in the world of tech support, I've gathered a wealth of knowledge and experiences. In this chapter, I want to share some practical tips that have proven invaluable in my tech support career. These tips, supported by examples and expert insights, can help you succeed in this ever-evolving field.

1. Be a Problem-Solver, Not a Troubleshooter

- *Tech support isn't just about fixing issues; it's about solving problems for users. Here are some practical tips for becoming an effective problem-solver:*

- *Ask Probing Questions: When a user reports an issue, it's essential to ask the right questions to gather all the necessary information. For example, if a user says, "My computer is slow," probing questions might include, "When did you first notice this issue, and does it happen with specific applications?" This technique helps uncover crucial details.*

- *Root Cause Analysis: Instead of treating the symptoms, focus on finding the root cause of the problem. For instance, if a user's email isn't working, consider whether it's a server issue, a misconfigured email client, or something else entirely. Identifying the root cause leads to more effective solutions.*

- *Documentation: Keep detailed records of the problems you encounter and the solutions you implement. This documentation can be invaluable for future reference and for training colleagues. As the management expert Peter Drucker once said, "What gets measured, gets managed." Documenting your work allows you to analyze trends and improve over time.*

2. Effective Communication is Key

Effective communication is the linchpin of tech support. Here are some practical tips for enhancing your communication skills:

- *Active Listening: Master the art of active listening by giving your full attention to users. Repeat back what you've heard to ensure clarity and demonstrate that you're engaged. As the psychologist Carl Rogers noted, "The major barrier to mutual interpersonal communication is our very natural tendency to judge, to evaluate, to approve or disapprove, the statement of the other person, or the other group."*

- *Use Plain Language: Avoid technical jargon when explaining solutions to users. Instead, use simple, everyday language that users can understand. As Albert Einstein wisely advised, "If you can't explain it simply, you don't understand it well enough."*

- *Empathy: Show empathy by acknowledging users' frustration or challenges. Phrases like "I understand how frustrating this must be" can go a long way in building rapport and trust. Psychologist Carl Rogers emphasized the importance of empathy in communication: "When someone really hears you without passing judgment on you, without trying to take responsibility for you, without trying to mold you, it feels damn good."*

3. Master Time Management

Time management is a critical skill in tech support, where multitasking and prioritization are essential. Here are some practical time management tips:

- *Prioritize Tasks: Start your day by identifying high-priority tasks and tackle them first. One valuable framework for prioritization is the Eisenhower Matrix, which categorizes tasks by urgency and importance. As Stephen Covey, author of "The 7 Habits of Highly Effective People," emphasized, "The key is not to prioritize what's on your schedule but to schedule your priorities."*

- *Time Blocking: Allocate specific blocks of time for different types of tasks. For example, reserve one block for responding to support tickets and another for proactive maintenance. Time blocking helps you maintain focus and avoid distractions, as advocated by productivity expert Cal Newport.*
- *Avoid Multitasking: Multitasking can lead to decreased efficiency and reduced quality of work. Focus on one task at a time to improve*

productivity and the quality of your support. As the psychologist Daniel Levitin pointed out, "Multitasking is the opportunity to screw up more than one thing at a time."

4. Embrace Change and Innovation

Tech support is a field that constantly evolves. Here are some practical tips for embracing change and fostering innovation:

- *Stay Informed: Regularly read tech blogs, attend webinars, and follow industry news to stay informed about emerging technologies and trends. As the tech visionary Steve Jobs noted, "Innovation distinguishes between a leader and a follower."*

- *Experiment: Don't be afraid to experiment with new support tools and methodologies. Test them in a controlled environment to see how they could improve your workflow. This experimental mindset aligns with the principles of design thinking, which encourages trying, testing, and iterating.*

- *User Feedback: Actively seek feedback from users about their support experience. Use this input to identify areas for improvement and innovation. Feedback loops are a fundamental part of the agile development methodology, which encourages continuous improvement based on user input.*

5. Cultivate a Growth Mindset

A growth mindset, the belief that abilities can be developed through dedication and hard work, is crucial for success in tech support. Here are some practical tips for cultivating a growth mindset:

- *View Challenges as Opportunities: When faced with a difficult problem, see it as a chance to learn and grow, rather than a roadblock. This perspective aligns with the growth mindset advocated by psychologist Carol Dweck.*

- *Seek Feedback: Embrace feedback as a tool for improvement. Ask colleagues for constructive feedback on your support techniques and communication. Feedback is an integral part of the continuous improvement process in lean and agile methodologies.*

- *Continuous Learning: Make lifelong learning a habit. Dedicate time each week to expand your knowledge in areas relevant to your role. This aligns with the principles of continuous improvement found in lean thinking and agile methodologies.*

These practical tips, grounded in our journey through the world of tech support, can serve as a compass to navigate the challenges and opportunities you'll encounter in your career. Remember that success in tech support is not just about technical skills but also about effective communication, adaptability, and a commitment to growth and improvement. With these principles in mind, you'll be well-equipped to excel in this dynamic and rewarding field. If you ever get stuck and do not know where to even start to fix an issue just remember the IT support basics I have illustrated on my next page.

CHAPTER 12:
THE JOURNEY AHEAD

As I conclude this book on succeeding in tech support, I find myself looking both backward and forward. We've covered a wide range of topics, from technical proficiency and communication to resilience, innovation, and the power of lifelong learning. It's been a journey filled with insights, experiences, and wisdom, and I hope you've found it as rewarding as I have.

Now, as we turn our gaze to the journey ahead, I want to leave you with some final thoughts and encouragement for your future in tech support.

Reflecting on Our Journey

Throughout this book, we've explored the multifaceted nature of tech support and the skills and qualities that can set you on a path to success. We've learned how technical expertise, effective communication, and time management are the foundational skills that support specialists rely on daily. We've also discussed the importance of resilience in the face of challenges and the role of innovation in shaping the future of tech support.

We've discovered that tech support is not just about solving technical problems but also about connecting with people, showing empathy, and building trust. The human side of tech support is a critical element that can make all the difference in the user's experience.

We've emphasized the importance of lifelong learning, inspired by the words of great minds like Albert Einstein and Steve Jobs. In a field that constantly evolves, your commitment to growth and adaptation is key to staying relevant and effective.

Your Unique Journey

As you move forward in your tech support career, remember that your journey will be unique. You'll encounter challenges and opportunities that are specific to your path. Embrace these experiences, learn from them, and continue to refine your skills and mindset.

Seek out mentors and colleagues who can offer guidance and support along the way. Collaboration and shared knowledge are powerful tools in the tech support world.

The Evolving Landscape

The tech support landscape will continue to evolve. New technologies will emerge, user expectations will change, and the tools and methods you use will adapt. Embrace these changes with an open mind and a willingness to explore. Remember that you have the capacity to shape the future of tech support through your innovation and dedication.

A Final Word of Encouragement

In closing, I want to remind you that tech support is a dynamic and rewarding field. It's a career that allows you to make a tangible impact on the lives of individuals and organizations. Your ability to solve problems, communicate effectively, and adapt to change will be invaluable assets in your journey ahead.

Never forget that every interaction with a user is an opportunity to not only resolve technical issues but also to build trust and leave a positive impression. Your role is essential, and your contributions matter.

As you step forward into the future of tech support, carry with you the knowledge and insights we've explored in this book. Embrace every challenge as an opportunity to grow, innovate, and excel. Your journey is just beginning, and the possibilities are limitless.

Thank you for joining me on this journey through the world of tech support. I wish you a fulfilling and successful career ahead, filled with growth, learning, and the satisfaction of making a difference in the world of technology and support.

WORKING IN IT CUSTOMER SUPPORT

MINDSET

- Be patient
- Politeness goes a long way
- Have a problem-solving attitude

SKILLS

- Communicate clearly
- Actively listen
- Adapt to new issues

WHAT TO EXPECT

- Technical problems to solve
- Upset or confused customers
- Learning continuously

RECOMMENDED KNOWLEDGE

- Operating systems
- Networking concepts
- Common software applications

CHAPTER 13:
ADVANCING YOUR TECH SUPPORT CAREER THROUGH COMPTIA CERTIFICATIONS

As we wrap up our journey through the world of tech support, I'd like to share some crucial steps that can help you advance in your career. One of the most effective ways to do so is by obtaining CompTIA certifications, particularly the A+, Network+, and Security+ certifications. These certifications are widely recognized in the IT industry and can open doors to new opportunities and increased earning potential.

Here are the steps to guide you in obtaining these valuable certifications:

Step 1: Define Your Career Goals

Before diving into certification preparation, it's essential to clarify your career goals. Are you aiming for a specific role in tech support, such as network administrator or cybersecurity specialist? Knowing your career objectives will help you choose the right certifications and tailor your study plan accordingly.

Step 2: Research CompTIA Certifications

CompTIA offers a range of certifications, but for tech support professionals, the A+, Network+, and Security+ certifications are highly relevant. Take the time to research each certification to understand its content, prerequisites, and potential career paths. Here's an overview:

- CompTIA A+ Certification: This certification validates foundational skills in IT, covering hardware, software, troubleshooting, and more. It's an excellent starting point for those new to tech support.

- CompTIA Network+ Certification: Network+ focuses on networking concepts, protocols, and best practices. It's ideal for those interested in network administration or support roles.

- CompTIA Security+ Certification: Security+ covers cybersecurity fundamentals, including threat detection, risk management, and encryption. It's essential for anyone pursuing a career in IT security.

Step 3: Create a Study Plan

Once you've chosen the certifications that align with your career goals, it's time to create a study plan. Break down your study schedule into manageable chunks, setting aside dedicated time for learning and exam preparation.

Step 4: Gather Study Materials

CompTIA offers official study materials, including textbooks and online courses, that are designed to align with their certification exams. Additionally, there are numerous third-party resources, such as books, video courses, and practice exams, that can aid in your preparation.

Step 5: Study Diligently

Commit to consistent and focused study. Utilize a variety of learning resources, including official CompTIA materials, books, video tutorials, and practice exams. Consider joining online forums or study groups to connect with others preparing for the same certifications.

Step 6: Hands-On Practice

Hands-on experience is invaluable in tech support. Set up a lab environment where you can practice the concepts and skills covered in your chosen certifications. Experiment with configuring networks, troubleshooting hardware issues, and implementing security measures.

Step 7: Take Practice Exams

Practice exams are excellent tools for gauging your readiness for the real certification exams. They simulate the testing environment and help you identify areas where you need further study. Many online platforms offer CompTIA practice exams.

Step 8: Register for Exams

Once you feel confident in your knowledge and skills, register for the official CompTIA exams. Be sure to review the exam objectives to ensure you've covered all the required topics.

Step 9: Exam Day Preparation

On the day of the exam, arrive early, well-rested, and with all necessary identification and paperwork. Take your time, read each question carefully, and don't rush. Remember that CompTIA exams are performance-based, so be prepared to demonstrate your practical skills.

Step 10: Continue Learning and Stay Updated

After achieving your CompTIA certifications, the learning journey doesn't end. The tech industry is ever-evolving, so staying updated is crucial. Engage in continuous learning through webinars, workshops, and advanced certifications in your chosen specialization.

By following these steps and obtaining CompTIA certifications, you'll not only enhance your knowledge and skills but also demonstrate your commitment to your tech support career. These certifications can open doors to new opportunities, higher salaries, and greater job satisfaction, making them valuable assets as you advance in your career.

APPENDIX A: SAMPLE TROUBLESHOOTING SCENARIOS

While it is hard to predict issues that may come up when you do tech support, there are issues you may see on a regular basis. I wanted to present you with three sample issues and troubleshooting steps to give you an idea of what you may come across. Just keep in mind that what ever the issue, effective communication, patience, and systematic problem-solving are key skills for resolving such problems efficiently and ensuring user satisfaction.

Scenario 1: Network Connectivity Issue

User Description: "I can't access the internet from my office computer. It was working fine this morning, but now I can't connect to any websites."

Troubleshooting Steps:

- *Ask the user to confirm if other colleagues are experiencing the same issue.*
- *Check if the network cable is securely connected to the computer and the wall socket.*

- *Verify that the network port on the computer is active and the network adapter is enabled in the device manager.*
- *Attempt to ping a known website (e.g., www.google.com) to check for DNS resolution issues.*
- *Restart the computer and test the internet connection again.*
- *If the issue persists, escalate the problem to network administrators or investigate if there are broader network issues.*

Scenario 2: Printer Not Printing

User Description: "I'm trying to print an important document, but my printer won't respond. It worked yesterday."

Troubleshooting Steps:

- *Confirm the printer is powered on and has paper and ink or toner.*
- *Check if there are any error messages or warning lights on the printer's control panel.*

- *Ensure the printer is set as the default printer on the user's computer.*
- *Check the print queue for any stuck print jobs. Cancel any pending print jobs if necessary.*
- *Restart both the computer and the printer.*
- *Test the printer with a simple document to see if it prints.*
- *If the issue persists, reinstall the printer drivers on the user's computer or consult the printer's manual for specific troubleshooting steps.*

Scenario 3: Email Account Access Issue

User Description: "I can't access my email. Every time I try to log in, it says my password is incorrect, but I haven't changed it."

Troubleshooting Steps:

- *Ask the user if they have tried resetting their password. If not, guide them through the password reset process.*
- *Confirm with the user that they are entering the correct username (email address) and password.*

- *Check if there are any system-wide email server issues affecting multiple users.*
- *Attempt to log in to the user's email account from an admin console to verify the account status and password.*
- *If necessary, unlock or reset the user's account and provide them with a temporary password.*
- *Instruct the user to change their password after successfully logging in.*
- *Provide guidance on setting up two-factor authentication for added security.*

APPENDIX B: GLOSSARY OF TECH SUPPORT TERMS

A list of technical terms and jargon

1. *Algorithm: A step-by-step set of instructions for solving a specific problem or performing a task.*
2. *API (Application Programming Interface): A set of rules and protocols that allows different software applications to communicate with each other.*
3. *Backup: A copy of data or files created to prevent data loss in case of system failure or accidental deletion.*
4. *Bandwidth: The maximum amount of data that can be transmitted over a network connection in a given time.*
5. *Browser: A software application used to access and view websites on the internet (e.g., Chrome, Firefox, Safari).*
6. *Cache: A temporary storage area where frequently accessed data is stored to improve system performance.*

7. *Cloud Computing: The practice of using remote servers hosted on the internet to store, manage, and process data and applications.*

8. *CPU (Central Processing Unit): The primary component of a computer responsible for executing instructions and performing calculations.*

9. *Database: A structured collection of data organized in a way that allows for efficient retrieval, storage, and manipulation.*

10. *DNS (Domain Name System): A system that translates human-readable domain names (e.g., www.example.com) into IP addresses used by computers to locate resources on the internet.*

11. *Firewall: A security system that monitors and controls incoming and outgoing network traffic to protect a network or computer from unauthorized access and threats.*

12. *Hardware: The physical components of a computer or electronic device, including the CPU, memory, keyboard, and monitor.*

13. *HTML (Hypertext Markup Language): The standard markup language used to create web pages.*

14. *HTTP (Hypertext Transfer Protocol): The protocol used for transferring data on the World Wide Web.*

15. *IP Address (Internet Protocol Address): A unique numerical label assigned to each device connected to a network to identify and locate it.*

16. *Malware: Software designed to harm, disrupt, or gain unauthorized access to computer systems or data, including viruses, worms, and spyware.*

17. *Operating System: Software that manages computer hardware and provides services for running applications (e.g., Windows, macOS, Linux).*

18. *Router: A device that directs data packets between different networks and enables devices to connect to the internet.*

19. *Software: Programs and applications that run on a computer or electronic device, such as word processors, web browsers, and games.*

20. *URL (Uniform Resource Locator): A web address that specifies the location of a resource on the internet.*

21. *Virus: Malicious software that can replicate and spread to other computers, often causing damage or stealing data.*

22. *Wi-Fi: A wireless technology that allows devices to connect to the internet without physical cables.*

23. *Encryption: The process of converting data into a code to protect it from unauthorized access.*

24. *LAN (Local Area Network): A network that connects devices within a limited geographic area, such as a home or office.*

25. *WAN (Wide Area Network): A network that spans a larger geographic area and connects multiple LANs.*

26. *URL: An acronym for "Uniform Resource Locator," it's the web address used to identify a resource on the internet.*

27. *Server: A computer or system that provides services or resources to other computers or devices on a network.*

28. *Browser Cookies: Small pieces of data stored on a user's computer by websites to track user activity and preferences.*

29. *Bluetooth: A wireless technology used for short-range communication between devices, such as smartphones, headphones, and speakers.*

30. *HTML: An acronym for "Hypertext Markup Language," it's the standard language used for creating web pages.*

31. *PDF (Portable Document Format): A file format used for documents that preserves their original appearance and layout, regardless of the software or hardware used to view them.*

32. *RAM (Random Access Memory): A type of computer memory used for storing data that is currently being used or processed.*

33. *URL: An acronym for "Uniform Resource Locator," it's the web address used to identify a resource on the internet.*

34. *WYSIWYG (What You See Is What You Get): An interface or editor that displays content as it will appear to the end user.*

35.*ZIP File: A compressed file format used to reduce the size of files and folders for easier storage and sharing.*

APPENDIX C:

The Following are several IT Training Posters I created to help explain some concepts you may come across in your IT Support Role.

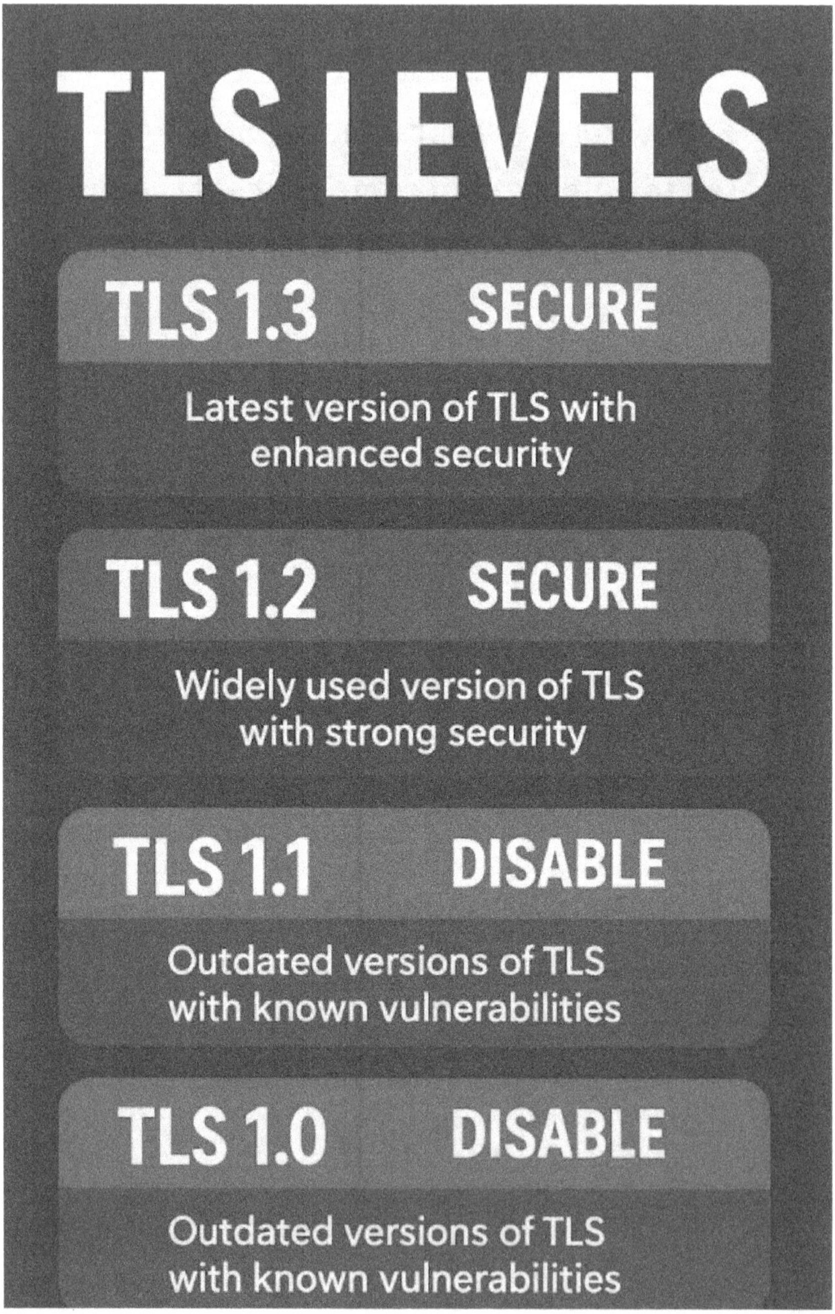
TLS LEVELS
TLS 1.3
SECURE
Latest version of TLS with enhanced security
TLS 1.2
SECURE
Widely used version of TLS with strong security
TLS 1.1
DISABLE
Outdated versions of TLS with known vulnerabilities
TLS 1.0
DISABLE
Outdated versions of TLS with known vulnerabilities

HTTP ERROR CODES

400
BAD REQUEST
The server could not
understand the request

401
UNAUTHORIZED
Authentication is required
to access the resource

403
FORBIDDEN
The server is refusing
to fulfill the request

404
NOT FOUND
The server cannot find the
requested resource

REAL-WORLD SCENARIOS FOR THE OSI MODEL

7 Application

6 Presentation

A user can't access a website

5 Session

Printer won't connect to the network

4 Transport

3 Network

VoIP calls are dropping or poor quality

2 Data Link

1 Physical

DISCLAIMER:

I want to make it clear that the information I provide is based on my knowledge and general understanding of the topics. It is intended for general informational purposes only and should not be considered professional advice I have been working in the field for over 20 years and it is ever changing and the one thing I can tell you is that you should never stop learning and do your best to stay current as this field never stops evolving.

I make every effort to ensure that the information I offer is accurate and up-to-date, but I cannot guarantee the accuracy, completeness, or suitability of the information for your specific situation. Any reliance you place on the information I provide is strictly at your own risk.

I do not endorse or recommend any specific products, services, or organizations unless explicitly stated. Any product or service recommendations are based on general knowledge and should not be seen as endorsements.

I am not liable for any losses, injuries, or damages arising from the use of the information provided. It is essential to consult with qualified professionals or experts for advice tailored to your unique circumstances.

Kind regards

Noe Tovar-MBA

In conclusion, " Tech Support Success Guide " is a call to action. It urges all of us to embrace the mindset of continuous learning, recognizing that the journey of self-improvement is ongoing. As the world evolves, so must our soft and hard skills. Through this exploration, my goal was to inspire readers to cultivate a holistic skill set that positions them not just as experts in their fields but as adept navigators of the complex, interconnected tapestry of modern Tech Support.

Kindest regards

Noe Tovar

SCAN FOR AUTHOR PAGE TO ACCESS
OTHER BOOKS BY THIS AUTHOR